| DATE DUE | | | 4 / 01 |
|---|---|---|---|
| APR 24 01 | | | |
| | | | |
| | | | |
| | | | |
| | | | |
| | | | |
| | | | |
| | | | |
| | | | |
| | | | |
| | | | |
| | | | |
| | | | |
| GAYLORD | | | PRINTED IN U.S.A |

# WILD BEARS!

# BLACK BEAR

**Text and Photographs by
Tom and Pat Leeson**

BLACKBIRCH PRESS, INC.

Published by Blackbirch Press, Inc.
260 Amity Road
Woodbridge, CT 06525

**Email:** staff@blackbirch.com
**Web site:** www.blackbirch.com

Printed in the United States

10 9 8 7 6 5 4 3 2 1

All photographs ©Tom and Pat Leeson.

**Library of Congress Cataloging-in-Publication Data**
Leeson, Tom.
Black bear / by Tom & Pat Leeson
        p. cm. — (Wild bears!)
    Includes index.
    Summary: Describes the physical appearance, habits, hunting and mating behaviors, family life, and life cycle of the black bear.
    ISBN 1-56711-343-5  (hardcover  : alk. paper)
    1. Black bear—Juvenile literature. [1. Black bear. 2. Bears.]  I. Leeson, Pat. II. Title.
    III. Series

QL737.C27 L42 2000
599.78'5—dc21                                                    00-008281

# Contents

# Introduction

Black bears roamed the forests of North America long before the Native Americans, the earliest-known settlers, arrived. And, unlike many animal species common at that time, black bear populations remain strong today.

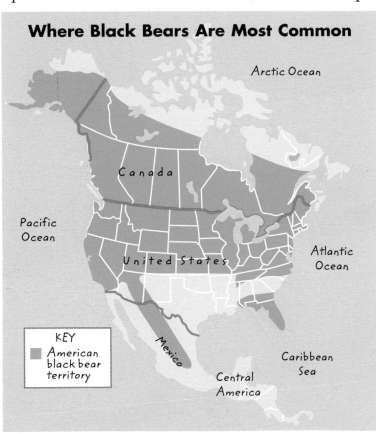

**Where Black Bears Are Most Common**

Arctic Ocean

Canada

Pacific Ocean

United States

Atlantic Ocean

Mexico

Caribbean Sea

Central America

KEY
American black bear territory

Scientists estimate that there are about 400,000 to 750,000 of the bears living in the wild.

Black bears are the most common of the 3 bear species living in North America. They are found in wooded areas all across the United States and Canada. They survive in many different habitats and climates, from steamy Mexico to icy Alaska. Black bears also inhabit many different forested areas, from Maine's hardwood forests to the swampy lowlands of Florida and Louisiana.

The other 2 kinds of bears that live in North America are polar bears and grizzly bears. Polar bears roam the Arctic sea ice, and grizzly bears like the open plains and treeless tundra (flat, open land).

Black bears live in a wide variety of climates and habitats.

# The Black Bear Body

Not all black bears are black. Most black bears found in the southwestern United States are the color of chocolate, cinnamon, or honey. Some black bears that live farther north—along the British Columbia coast—are even a creamy white color! Black bears that are found in the Smoky Mountains, the Appalachian Mountains, and the Great Lakes region usually have black fur coats.

A black bear has a large, wedge-shaped head. On top of its head are 2 round ears that can swivel slightly to help the animal locate sound. Black bears can hear better than humans. They see in color, and have good vision at close range.

**Top:** Some of the black bears that live on the coast of British Columbia are white.
**Bottom:** Black bears can rotate their ears to locate sounds.
**Opposite:** When it prepares for hibernation, a black bear's weight can double.

An adult black bear is 5 to 6 feet (1.5 to 1.8 meters) long. When it stands on its 4 legs, this bear is 2 to 3 feet (61 to 91 centimeters) high at its front shoulders. Most adult black bears weigh between 130 to 500 pounds (59 to 227 kilograms). A black bear's weight changes dramatically through-out the year. It can weigh 150 pounds (68 kilograms) in the spring, and double its weight by fall before it hibernates (sleeps for winter). Usually, males are larger than females, and eastern bears are larger than their western cousins.

All bears have wide, flat paws with 5 toes. Black bears seldom, if ever, walk on their hind legs like circus bears. When they are disturbed or frightened, they will stand on their hind legs to see over bushes and shrubs. They will also stand on their hind legs to reach berries or fruit hanging from trees.

Even with their large size and relatively short legs, black bears are fast runners. Over short distances, they can reach up to 25 miles (40 kilometers) per hour.

**Left:** Black bears stand on their hind legs to reach hanging fruit and to see over bushes.
**Opposite:** When they are threatened, black bears often climb trees.

# Special Features

A black bear's short, sharp claws are important to its survival. Full-grown adults have few natural enemies. One of their most dangerous enemies is the grizzly bear. A black bear often climbs a tree when it is threatened. Its sharp claws dig into the tree bark and allow the animal to quickly climb to safety. Because grizzlies have longer claws, they are unable to follow black bears up tree trunks. As long as black bears remain close to wooded areas, they are generally safe from attack.

A black bear's keen sense of smell also helps it to stay safe and find food. A bear is able to smell 12 to 15 times better than a human! This is because its long snout is filled with olfactory (smelling) nerves that cover about 100 times more surface area than in a human nose. On a damp, windy day, a black bear can smell ripe berries or rotting meat several miles away.

**Left:** A black bear's sharp claws can dig into tree bark.
**Above:** To find food, bears rely on their strong sense of smell.

# Hibernation

One of the black bear's most unique features is its ability to hibernate (stay in a sleeplike state). Because food is scarce in winter, most black bears hibernate. In the fall, a bear searches for a den. Sometimes it digs an underground sleeping room by enlarging an old coyote den. Other times, it finds a hollow log and crawls inside. Some bears even sleep underneath the porches of summer cabins!

A black bear can sleep for months at a time. Once it hibernates, its body temperature drops about 10 degrees. To survive without eating, a bear uses the fat it has stored up. Some bears that live in the South only hibernate for 1 or 2 months. Bears that live in colder locations may hibernate for up to 7 months, usually from October to April. During hibernation, a bear may lose 25% or more of its weight.

When it is ready to hibernate in the fall, a black bear searches for a den.

11

# Social Life

A male black bear (called a boar) spends most of his life alone. A female (called a sow) spends most of her life raising her cubs. The female's only break usually comes after her older cubs have left her and she is preparing to give birth again.

A sow often has small cubs that depend on her to find food for them. Because of this, she has a set territory called a home range. These territories vary in size from 3 to 10 sq. miles (7 to 26 sq. kilometers). Although males may wander through some 40 sq. miles (124 sq. kilometers) or more to known food sources, a mother bear's ability to travel is limited by the age and strength of her cubs.

A male black bear lives alone, except during mating season.

Black bears will fight for their home ranges if food is scarce.

All adult black bears have a home territory. The size of the territory and how strongly they defend it depends on how much food the area produces. If it is a rich food area, a bear will have a smaller territory, and it doesn't need to defend the area as aggressively. If food is scarce, a bear will fight strongly to defend its home range.

Adult black bears generally do not mix together, except for brief times during mating season. When there is a lot of food in one area, they may make an exception. Sometimes, groups can be seen fishing along a stream that is full of salmon.

Where there is plenty of fish, black bears sometimes gather in groups to feed.

Because there is more than enough fish for all of the bears to eat, the animals generally will not fight with one another. Sometimes, however, younger bears may have to give up a good fishing spot to a larger, older bear.

# Hunting and Food

Like most humans, black bears are omnivores. This means they eat both plants and animals. In the spring, when they first come out of hibernation, most black bears feed heavily on grass and new plant growth. Some scientists believe this plant diet helps clean out a bear's digestive system. This prepares a black bear for the heavy eating it needs to do to get ready for next year's hibernation.

Black bears do not have strong hunting skills. They sometimes prey on other animals in late spring or early summer, when the forests are full of young deer and elk.

In early spring, plants and grasses make up most of a black bear's diet.

Bears in other habitats catch fish. On the West Coast, spawning salmon or suckers are easy for black bears to catch in small streams.

During the summer, black bears eat many kinds of insects. They catch ants, pick caterpillars and grasshoppers off plants, and tear old logs apart looking for grubs (insect larvae) in the soft wood.

Black bears that live on the West Coast like to eat salmon.

Black bears always seem to be hungry—so they're always on the lookout for a big meal. In late summer and early fall, they enter a super-eating mode called hyperphagia (hi•per•fáy•sha). The bears eat all the time, taking only brief naps. During hyperphagia, a bear may consume over 20,000 calories per day!

In August and September, a black bear may gain 75 to 150 pounds (34 to 68 kilograms) as it prepares for hibernation. To gain weight fast, most black bears stuff themselves with nuts and berries. Bears that find high-fat acorns, beechnuts, or pine nuts put on the most weight. Bears that eat only low-fat berries like mountain ash, huckleberries, buffalo berries, and other fruit must eat more to store up fat for hibernation.

**Above:** Eating lots of nuts and seeds helps a black bear gain weight quickly.
**Below:** During summer, black bears feed constantly to prepare for hibernation.

# The Mating Game

Black bears mate in June. Sows that live in areas where food is plentiful may be ready to mate when they are between the ages of 2 and 3. Females living where food is scarce may not be ready to have young until they are 6 or even 7 years old.

A female's mating season begins when she pushes her grown cubs away to live on their own. Then, the female is ready to find a mate. Her body produces a scent that tells male bears she is ready.

A male finds a female by using his strong sense of smell. Once he has found a mate, the pair stays together for 3 or 4 days.

Sometimes several males may be drawn to the same female. Usually the most aggressive or largest male scares off the other males. He does this by making huffing noises, or by tearing up a log or tree. If this doesn't scare off the other males, then the bears may fight. The winner will mate with the female.

After mating, the male and female part ways. The male does not help the female raise the cubs. In fact, he may father cubs with several females during the same mating season.

**Opposite:** Black bears stay together for 3 or 4 days after they mate.
**Right:** If a female attracts several suitors, the most aggressive male scares the others away.

# Cubs

Black bear cubs are born in January and early February while their mother is hibernating in her den. At birth, the hairless cubs weigh 6 to 12 ounces (170 to 340 grams) and are about 9 inches (23 centimeters) long. Generally 2 or 3 cubs are born in a litter, but sows with 5 or 6 cubs have been seen. Usually, a female's litter size increases as she gets older.

Cubs are not able to see until they are about 6 weeks old, but they use their sharp claws to pull themselves into their mother's warm, furry folds of skin. The young cubs will stay there for the next 3 to 4 months, drinking their mother's rich milk and staying warm.

**Far left:** Cubs climb trees to escape danger.
**Left:** Cubs first leave the den in the spring.

When the cubs leave the den in mid-to-late spring, they weigh about 8 pounds (3.6 kilograms). For the next few months, these small animals are in danger of becoming a tasty meal for wolves, coyotes, and other bears. Cubs quickly learn to climb trees when danger threatens. The mother bear will defend her young by charging and snapping her teeth.

Cubs travel with their mother throughout the summer and fall. They learn how to catch fish and where to find ripe berries and fallen nuts. In the fall cubs hibernate with their mother. When spring comes, the growing cubs once again travel with their mother in search of food. After a month or two, they are big enough to live on their own. Their mother begins to snap, growl, and chase them away so she can prepare for another mating season and a new family.

**Top:** A mother black bear teaches her cubs many important skills.
**Bottom:** A young cub waits in a safe place as its mother searches for a meal.

21

# Bears and Humans

Humans have always been a black bear's main predator. During the settlement of North America, many bears were hunted. Bear fat was also commonly used as cooking oil.

Today, many people fear bears. Black bears, however, rarely attack humans. In the last 100 years, only 30 people have been killed by black bears. Although the bears are big and powerful, they usually avoid people.

The Biggest Problem between bears and humans is our food—the taste of it is irresistible to bears. When people bring food into forests and parks, bears can smell it. Even empty wrappers have a strong scent to a bear. When bears get a taste of human food, they can become dangerous. Sometimes animals must be moved to a new location so they will not injure people in their effort to get more human food.

Black bears have adapted to the large numbers of people living in North America. They are not endangered. They should continue to survive as long as humans continue to respect their habitat and their special way of life.

**Opposite:** Black bears love to eat human food and will pick through garbage to get it.
**Inset:** A tree that has been stripped by bears.

# Bear Facts

**Name:** Black Bear

**Scientific Name:** Ursus americanus

**Shoulder Height:** 2–3 feet (35–92 centimeters)

**Body length:** 5–6 feet (150–180 centimeters)

**Tail length:** 4–5 inches (12 centimeters)

**Weight:** Females—90–300 pounds (41–136 kilograms); males—200–600 pounds (91–272 kilograms). Cub at birth—8 ounces (227 grams)

**Color:** Black, chocolate, cinnamon, honey, creamy white

**Reaches Sexual Maturity:** 4 to 5 years

**Females mate:** Usually every 2 years

**Gestation:** About 220 days, but because of delayed implantation, the embryo only develops the last 10 weeks

**Litter size:** 1 to 5 (usually 2 to 3)

**Favorite Foods:** Honey, fish, berries, nuts, carrion (dead animals)

**Habitat:** Forested areas throughout the continental United States, Mexico, and Canada

**Life span:** 20 to 30 years

# Glossary

**climate** The usual weather in a place.

**habitat** The place and natural conditions in a which an animal or plant lives.

**hibernation** Spending the winter in a deep sleep to survive low temperatures and limited food.

**olfactory** Having to do with the sense of smell.

**predator** An animal that hunts other animals for food.

**prey** An animal that is hunted by another animal for food.

**territory** An area of land in which a certain animal or species is found.

# For More Information

## Books

Bailey, Donna. *Bears* (Animal World). Chatham, NJ: Steck-Vaughn Library, 1998.

Clark, Margaret Goff. *The Threatened Florida Black Bear.* New York, NY: Cobblehill, 1995.

Hunt, Joni Phelps. *Bears: A Global Look at Bears in the Wild.* Morristown, NJ: Silver Burdett Press, 1995.

## Web Site

*The Bear Den*

Find out interesting information on many species of bears, including their habitat, hunting and feeding behaviors, cubs, and survival in the wild—*www.naturenet.com/bears/*

# Index